PIECES
of
MIND

A.A. WINSTON

Pieces of Mind
Copyright © 2023 by A.A. Winston

ISBN: 978-1639457571 (sc)
ISBN: 978-1639457588 (e)

Writers' Branding
(877) 608-6550
www.writersbranding.com
media@writersbranding.com

CONTENTS

Dedication v

Introduction vii

An Ode: Mr. Jones, an Adaption* 1

Anguish 3

Living a Country Song 5

When I Want 7

Collapse 9

Breaking the Bond 11

Just the Messenger 13

Fortunes 14

9/11 16

Making Me Happy 18

The Drive 20

In a Basket 22

Behind Closed Doors 23

In These Days 25

Not a Hero 27

Backburner 28

Cliché (News Media) 29

Half-Life 30

Self Portrait 31

Coming 32

Hopes 33

Mania 34

Gotta Be Kidding 35

Immortalized 36

Cantankerous Man 37

Cliché (Sports) 38

Sign 40

Peace and Therapy 41

Sound of Fury 42

Overused 43

Magic 45

Merry Little Last K Home Game* 46

Rest Now 47

Rock 'N' Roll Poet 48

Message Received 49

Yours to Finish 51

All Balled Up 52

Slippery Slope 53

Sandy Hook, Now Uvalde 55

Traitor 56

I See Black 58

Autobiography 59

Let Freedom Wring 61

'20 62

Apologies 63

Same Coin 64

Son of Mine 65

Three Dads 66

No Regrets................................68

Right and Wrong Speech 70

Hindsight 72

What a Ball................................73

Another Ho Hum Day 74

Lost Boys................................75

Best Love Song 76

Whore-ifying 77

The Moment................................78

Bridges and Arcs 79

Residuals................................80

Crossfire 81

Mural................................82

Club 83

Percent of Forever 84

Expiration Date 85

DEDICATION

This volume of poems is dedicated to everyone who has seen me through to this point. Many people have come through my life. Some have passed through, some have stayed. Some gave me confidence, some stepped on it. Extra credit goes to my mother, wife, son and siblings.

For those who are constants and those who are not, you all shaped me one way or another. I still have things you've said, done, and given in my head and heart. You have made me what I am for better or worse. I am grateful for you being part of my life because whether it was positive or negative you still contributed to my experiences and viewpoints.

INTRODUCTION

My first book, *Growth,* was for me. I had to prove that I could expose my feelings and put out all the poems I had been working on for almost 40 years. That span covered from my teenage years to middle age. It was an ending point as well as a starting point.

Once I was able to release all that pent up poetry, it seemed a new flow began. I looked at things around me differently and much of what is in *Pieces of Mind* are observations and my reactions to current events and things happening around me.

The works in *Pieces of Mind* contain tributes to those who had or continue to have profound impact on my life. There are also many takes on the tumultuous world we now live, including politics, media, and general societal behaviors.

As you read these poems, my hope is to provoke thought. I like to think of this book as full of healthy skepticism. Opinion is intertwined within the poetry, and I do not expect everyone to agree with what I offer. But if they get you to ask a question or two of yourself then I have made a connection somehow, someway.

AN ODE: MR. JONES, AN ADAPTATION*

I was down by the Lake Sebago
In my Father's House.
Staring at this brown-haired girl.
Mr. Jones strikes up a conversation.
Have I told you this story?
Tell me if I'm repeating myself
As he chews on his Neccos.

Jerry Sparks and a host of tacklers - 9
Julius revering Neibuhr
Ernie and his gifted craftsmanship
Squeak shooting through the kitchen window
DW and the Goldkist, brilliant as it be
Mama Carol traipsing with delight.

Mr. Jones donning his Chinese Devils cap
Nancy in her bun
Arcs as strong as ever
Margie with her father/daughter Duke days
Rachel competing in her tennis tourneys
Brooks making puns all the way.

It all meant something before
Now it means all the more.

Here's to you, David Jones
Jesus loves you more than you will know
God bless you, please, David Jones
Heaven holds a place for those who pray.

Where have you gone, David Jones?
Our family turns its lonely eyes to you.
Bend your knees
Follow through
Everything will be ok.
Hey, hey, hey
Hey, hey, hey.

*Source material: Here's to You, Mrs. Robinson by Simon & Garfunkel and Mr. Jones by Counting Crows

ANGUISH

I love you with everything I got.
I've always fought for you.
Always have, always will.
I've been there for you.
Every step of the way.

That won't change,
But I won't sit back and take this abuse.
It is uncalled for
There is no reason for this hostility.

We have things to work on together
But if you want to be treated
Like an adult
Behave like one.

Part of that is having
Conversations face to face.
You may not like
How those conversations go
But that's how you work things out.

Tough situations
Tough discussions
We all get frustrated,
Annoyed, and angry.
That stands for everyone.

I'm only human
Like you.
I'm not perfect.
Never said I was.

I take responsibility
For everything I have done
Or should have handled better.

But it's a two-way street
That comes around.
While it takes three to tango
It takes two to dance.

LIVING A COUNTRY SONG

Lost my job.
My car broke down.
My love is miles away.
My boy lives up north.

Trying to have a little hope
While living a country song.

My house needs new floors.
The back deck is falling apart.
My lawnmower don't work.
I have a crick in my neck.

Trying to have a little hope
While living a country song.

The world is ablaze with hate.
Fighting in the streets.
Black versus white.
Every shade in between.

Trying to have a little hope
While living a country song.

Politicians and press stir the pot.
Keep people apart.
Red versus blue.
Who's willing to tell the truth?

Trying to have a little hope
While living a country song.

Bots leaving bait.
Falling into traps.
Smart versus not.
Misinformed all the way around.

Trying to have a little hope
While living a country song.

Kneeling out of protest.
Kneeling out of prayer.
Humanity versus hypocrisy.
What in Hell is the God we seek?

Trying to have a little hope
While living a country song.

I still don't have a job.
My car still doesn't work.
I don't even have a dog.
He died a couple years ago.
I can only wallow in my beer . . .

Trying to have a little hope
While living a country song . . .
Living a country song . . .
Living a country song . . .
Living a country . . .
Living a . . .
Living . . .

WHEN I WANT

I can be prolific
When I want.
I can procrastinate
When I don't.

I can have my starts
When I want.
I can have my fits
When I don't.

I can walk the straight
When I want.
I can walk the narrow
When I don't.

I can pick my battles
When I want.
I can watch my back
When I don't.

I can go round in circles
When I want.
I can chase my tail
When I don't.

I can't see you
When I want.
I can't touch you
When I want.
I can't talk to you
When I want.

I can be with you in my mind
When you want.
I can be with you in my heart
When you want.
I can be with you in my soul
When you want.

COLLAPSE

Pushing.
Pulling.

Never at rest.

Pumping.
Pressing.

Never at rest.

Pacing.
Chasing.

Never at rest.

Thinking.
Speaking.

Never at rest.

Stretching.
Breaking.

Never at rest.

Dipping.
Dropping.

Never at rest.

Slipping.
Falling.

Never at rest.

Crashing.
Stopping.

Rest in peace.

BREAKING THE BOND

You tried 'so hard
To break the bond
Between father and son.

But you couldn't get it done.

You called the shots
With minions in tow
Using surprise as a weapon
Seemingly thinking one step ahead.

Always the victim
Never the attacker
Staging confrontation
To keep up with appearances.

You tried so hard
To break the bond
Between father and son.

But you couldn't get it done.

You didn't count
On me staying in the game
You thought erroneously
That you could outlast me.

Yet, you haven't learned your lesson
As you continue to connive
We're here for the distance
He and I.

You tried so hard
To break the bond
Between father and son.

But you couldn't get it done.

JUST THE MESSENGER

Sitting with my privilege
With a thumb up my ass
Tired of the rhetoric
Swirling all around.

Don't ask me to intervene.
The sidelines offer too much derision.
Don't understand what you mean.
When the system is broken.

Economically,
Educationally,
Legally.

Without equality,
Without equity,
Without diversity,
Without inclusivity.

Brand me a bigot?

Yes, you are.

Even I
Sitting with my privilege
With a thumb up my ass
Can see that far.

FORTUNES

It's funny how quickly
Fortunes turn.
At one moment,
You can be crushed by something
That brought high hopes
Of being the ultimate relationship
The pinnacle of everything you have strived for
Waiting years to reach
What you thought many times was unreachable
But always had in the back of your mind.

I loved her
She loved me
Arguably, we still love each other.
I don't know if this has been
Harder on me or her
Seems she can't let go
Maybe she didn't have an alternative
Maybe she didn't count on my agreeing
With her summation
That it was the best thing for both of us
Maybe we'll never know.

But out of that crushing blow
Came a sort of renewal
I'm not very religious,
But might be on the spiritual
I am a believer of things
Happening for a reason
For better or worse

And out of the worse
Finding the blade of positive
That moves life from backward
To neutral
And forever forward.

And then you turn a corner
Take a peek at what's on the other side
You find out the grass
On a relative term
Is greener.

We found out the what if
Maybe we were lucky
A lot of people never go back
To satisfy that question.
We took the opportunity.
We should be proud
Of that fact, at the very least.
The answer was what we expected,
But the question was answered.
It turned out to be
A what isn't and won't be.

It allowed us,
Perhaps me,
To move on.
I needed to see
What I really wanted.
More importantly
What I needed.

9/11

I didn't lose anybody,
But on that day
I believe we all lost something.
We chose the wrong path as a result.
One could say the architects,
Accomplished their mission.

Time has passed.
We have cratered as a people,
And as a country.
They wanted us to lose faith
In our institutions,
And our people.

When we should have stayed
We strayed.

As I hear and see the victims' names
Flash across the television screen,
I see a range of ages,
A spectrum of nationalities
And races
And the breadth of religions.

I see the legacy of immigrants.
I see the true representation of America.
I see us.

I hearken to harness
The unity we felt,
The unity we shared,
The unity we experienced,
That day in 2001
Seemingly momentarily
As the weeks passed.

When I see the blue ribbons
Worn by families and dignitaries
Honoring the memories
Of those who died,
And the unity we possess
For a few ephemeral hours each 9/11,
I see opportunity
I see a chance
To change the trajectory
A chance to right the wrongs,
Expose the truths
Of our past and present
So that we may seize
A stronger future.

Would this not be
The best way
to honor the victims?

Shouldn't that be
The legacy
Of that fateful day?

MAKING ME HAPPY

On a late afternoon
On a sunny, warm day
When he was eight
Don't know If he wanted to be there
But he was there with me.

We found our seats
In the right field bleachers
Overlooking the greenest of grasses
The tallest of green walls.
Don't know if he wanted to be there
But he was there with me.

Came down
To a place called Pesky's Pole
Hoping to be noticed
As he stood quietly
Amid a screaming and waving crowd.
Don't know if he wanted to be there
But he was there with me.

When a forgotten player
From another land
Came strolling over
With a ball in hand.
He reached out to him
And handed him the souvenir.
Don't know if he wanted to be there
But he was there with me.

A special moment
Followed by a Big Papi homer.
Highlights of a day
Shared by father and son.
Don't know if he wanted to be there
But he was there with me.

THE DRIVE

Pancakes and sausage
To start the day.
A promise of an eclipse
As one rite
Overshadowed by the next.

A passage of time.
Signs and markers
Landmarks rise and fall.

A cloudy day
As we rode down the highway.
Hid the dimness of the sun.

Your years increase.
A counting ritual
Celebrating your birth.

Lines guiding northward
Slithering from the south
Westerly winds in a sideways breeze.

Dots of destinations
Small and large
Stopping for rest and restoration.

Winding their way
Toward a final destination
Curved roads and wide lanes.

At the end of the road
You took a turn
Down life's thoroughfare
From boy to man.

IN A BASKET

In a basket
He arrived.
Mother to lawyer
Lawyer to mother
Be a good boy,
She said,
As he lay.

In a basket
Something to behold.
Mother to father
Father to son
A case to behold
You've been a good boy.

Hear her say
Mother to son
As if proving a prophecy
From a basket
You've always been a good boy.

BEHIND CLOSED DOORS

I want something
Left to imagination.

Don't need open doors
To things I don't want to see.

Don't need to see the pages
Of your open book.

Don't need to see
What you do at home
Behind closed doors.

Don't need the intimate details
From your intimate antics.

Don't care what you do
In the bedroom.
Or the maladies you suffer.
How you're leaking.
What's spitting out your mouth.
What's spewing out your butt.

Don't need to see your panties.
Nor your bras,
Your bulges,
And crooked carrots.

Give me some humility.
Give me some tight lips
That don't sink ships.

Don't need more open windows
To your birthday suit
Keep it in your pants
Behind closed doors.

IN THESE DAYS

Not enough power
To go around
Scrounging for the bits
The crumbs at the tips.

Wish I had died in the cradle
To see the world I see today.

Investing in the people
Is a poor investment for some.
Rolling back the times
In hopes of collecting some dimes.

Wish I had died in the cradle
To see the world I see today.

Depleting a democracy
While lifting an autocracy.
Step on many
On high from a few.

Wish I had died in the cradle
To see the world I see today.

Looking down from above
Lofty positions they keep.
A broken ladder
Fulfilled through deceit.

Wish I had died in the cradle
To see the world I see today.

On prayer they stand
With guns to their head.
Shoot to kill the children.
Unthinkable thoughts in these days.

Wish I had died in the cradle
To see the world I see today.

NOT A HERO

He was not a hero.
Just a man.
He had his fallacies.
He had his faults.

Not too perfect
No man can.
He stretched the truth,
Almost on command.

He tried his best.
Like any man
He had limitations.
Some I'll never understand.

Time doesn't stand still
For any man.
Bound by heredity,
Not realized on demand.

Reminded of mortality
Fate of all man.
Blinded by the shortcomings,
Intensified through reprimand.

He was not a hero.
A man after all.
Despite the weaknesses
He still stands tall.

BACKBURNER

Put your hopes
On the backburner.
Put your dreams
On the backburner.
Put your self-pity
On the backburner.
Put your victimhood
On the backburner.

CLICHÉ (NEWS MEDIA)

Tip of the spare
Conflate
Breaking news
Doubling down
High stakes
Crisis/crises
Existential threats
Inflection point
Knife's edge
Unprecedented
Bombshell
So much at stake.

Word of the day
Phrase of the month
Hysteria of the moment.

Tell me what to say.
Tell me what to think.
Tell me what I want to hear.
Tell me, tell me,
Because I can't think for myself.

Pit us against each other.
Over the latest faux difference
Tell us we can't agree.

For the sake of a shareholder
Tell me who I should believe.
Decide for me who I should despise.

HALF-LIFE

12 plus years
152 months
7,904 weeks
55,328 days
1,327,872 hours

A full life if I had the chance.

6 plus years
76 months
3,953 weeks
27,664 days
669,936 hours

Half a life with the chance given.

So much time
Taken away
So much time
I would have had.
Time so precious
I can never get back.

Oh, what I missed
I'll always know
Oh, what you missed
You can't tell.

A whole life is what's left.

SELF PORTRAIT

Self portrait
Sitting on the dresser.
So pensive.
So insecure.

Self portrait
Sitting on the dresser.
So scared.
So introspective.

Self portrait
Sitting on the dresser.
So full of doubt.
So full of mystery.

Self portrait
Sitting on the dresser.
Staring at me daily.
Dressing me down.

Self portrait
Sitting on the dresser.
Did I put you there?
Are you full of despair?

COMING

I came to you
When things were bad
Then things got worse
Not much of a fairy tale.

Dragon my tail
Between my legs
As I cruise
Past your door.

A train wreck
Between my ears
Going through life
On a whistle-stop tour.

Banging my head
Against the wall
Dazed by the gains
Of dispensing you.

Nobody noticed
Because
Of the confusion
On my face.

I escaped
But nobody knew
All they saw
Was the chalk outline
Of a time gone by.

HOPES

We pin our hopes
On days to come
Of things we said
On things we did.

When twinkles in our eyes grew.
From infants
To toddlers
To adolescents
To young adults.

Living off our wisdom
For better or worse.
We hope they pass along
Beyond ourselves
Days of yore.

MANIA

Manic moments
Emitting from my brain.
Transmissions devolve
To where I cannot sleep.
Electric waves evolve
To euphoric heights.

GOTTA BE KIDDING

You've gotta be kidding
What did I just hear?
What did I just see?
I can't believe what I just heard.
I can't believe what I just saw.

Do you expect me to believe
What I just heard?
Do you expect me to believe
What I just saw?

What nonsense you say!
What nonsense you do!

You can gaslight.
You can ghost.
But I know what you're about.

I have my own ears.
I have my own eyes.
I know what I hear.
I know what I see.

IMMORTALIZED

I've been immortalized
In the pages of newsprint.
Learned things I didn't know
Met people I preferred not to.
Asked a lot of questions
Aimed at the truth.
Hidden agendas
Dissected situations.
Tutored by mentors
Guided by sources.
Taken in
Wrung out.
Cups and cups of coffee
Each and every day.
What's black and white
And read all over?
Stop the presses
On a breaking moment.
Woman stabbed,
Restaurant robbed,
Building on fire.
Name is all you got
At the top of the page
Nobody talks
If you bury the lede.
When you are immortalized.

CANTANKEROUS MAN

Pfft.
Huff.
Ugh.
Oy.
Grrr.

Get off my lawn.
Get out of my way.
Turn down the noise.
Turn up the volume.

I'm a cantankerous man
Who can't understand
How I got left behind.
When I was so young
I was so hip
Squared by the knowledge
Of what I didn't know.

CLICHÉ (SPORTS)

Pitch and catch.
Tip your cap.
A bunch of warriors
Ready to go to battle.

They battled hard,
But we stuck together.
We love each other.
Like brothers
We are a family
Bonded by a singular mission.

At the end of the day
We came out ahead
Taking one day at a time
We'll keep fighting
For another day.

Thank my teammates.
Thank my coaches.
Thank the fans.
The best anywhere.

But most of all
Thank my family
And Jesus above
Without them
I wouldn't be here.

I can't say enough.
In the end
I gave it my all
With a mouth
Full of buzzwords.

SIGN

Waiting for a sign from above.
Looking deep
Into the underground.
Stuck in the purgatory of life.
With a high-altitude attitude
In the depths of Hell.

PEACE AND THERAPY

Slam.
Trash.
Demolish.
Take a hammer.
Smash it up.
Give me some peace
With this therapy.
Something to be said
For creating serenity
Through chaotic means.

SOUND OF FURY

Musicians mumbling
Into a microphone
Garbled words
With cliché meanings
Generic lines
Meant to mesmerize.
Thunderously a-symphonic
Noticeably pretentious
Supposedly anthemic
Needlessly narcissistic.

Enchanting,
Opulent,
Untethered melodies.
Luminous grooves,
Cascading piano lines,
Soaring vocals,
Flowery and frivolous,
All at the same time.
No real significance
Simply deep meaningless.

OVERUSED

Hero, Great, Expert, Love
Overused and overstated.

Hero -
Need more than signing up.
Need more than a uniform.
Need more than a flag.
Need more than a tour of duty.
To earn the label
Of hero.

Great -
Need more than just showing up.
Need more than a little sweat.
Need more than minimal effort.
Need more than one success.
To earn the label
Of great.

Expert –
Need more than a piece of paper.
Need more than a book.
Need more than a podcast.
Need more than a brain.
To earn the label
Of expert.

Love -
Need more than being present.
Need more than a passing glance.

Need more than a kiss.
Need more than a brief encounter.
To earn the label
Of love.

MAGIC

Abracadabra
They don't like you
Using their tricks.
Behind the smiles
Sleight of hand.
Artistry at work
Without a conscience.
They make you believe
What you see is unreal.

MERRY LITTLE LAST K HOME GAME*

Have yourself a merry little last K home game
Let your heart be light.
From now on
Your troubles will be out of sight.

Have yourself a merry little last K home game
Make the Cameron Crazies gay.
From now on
Your troubles will be miles away.

Here we are as in the olden days.
Happy golden days of yore
Faithful friends who are dear to us
They gather near to us once more.

Dave and Nancy through the years
The Dawkins, Laettner, Hill and Boozer
Kyrie's lone worthy contribution
A first date to remember.

We'll always be together.
Cut the nets down at the ACC.
If the Fates allow
Hang a shiny banner from the highest beam.

And have yourself a merry little last K home game.
Have yourself a merry little last K home game.
So have yourself a merry little last K home game*.

Source: Merry Little Christmas

REST NOW

Settle down.
Storm is over.
Swirling winds.
Heavy downpours.
I could die tonight
Knowing I dang done my best.

Rest now
You are home.
Unchained from entanglements,
Free from the disillusions,
Not scared by the hallucinations,
That seem so vivid in your mind.

Time to relax.
Lay your head down.
Sleep peacefully.
You've earned
A reprieve
From life's constant bombardments.

Close your eyes.
Nothing more to think about.
Let your heart slow down
To a peaceful rate.
One that you can never repeat.

ROCK 'N' ROLL POET

Destroyed by love
So, what?

Pick yourself up
No skin off your teeth
Defiant as they come
As a rock 'n' roll poet
Nothing gets in your way.

Dig in your heels.
Scream to a shout.
The guitars are blaring.
The drums are snaring.
Triumphant without a care.

As the saying goes,
If I knew then
What I know now
I'd be dangerous
In a world that gets in my way.

MESSAGE RECEIVED

I can hear your call
No matter how close
Or how far.

I can hear the alarm
In your voice
Strained and stressed.

I can hear your call
No matter how close
Or how far.

I can't see you,
But I can feel you.
Like the reverb of a guitar
The bang of a drum
Ripples of vibes
Racing through my brain
Sending shocks through my system.

I can hear your call
No matter how close
Or how far.

Minds in tune
Senses on alert
A break in the force
From deep inside
I can't reach you,
But I feel you

As if you are standing
Right by my side.

I can hear your call
No matter how close
Or how far.

YOURS TO FINISH

People knowing things unknown
Tend to make the most of everything.
Feeble jealousies supplant rationale,
Stripping man of all his pride.
The last word is always sought...

ALL BALLED UP

Crumpled in the fetal position
Petrified like a possum
On the side of the road
Roadkill never had it so easy.

I have to come clean.
There were many times
I wished she'd go away.

I'd warp my time
To get ahead
From where I've been.

SLIPPERY SLOPE

We hear the argument all the time -
Can't restrict guns
Because that's a slippery slope.

Age rules,
Required training,
Background checks,
Red flags.

Black flags
That lead down
A slippery slope – they say.

Don't have much to say
As children die in their seats,
Those of color die in the streets.

Good guys with guns
Protect us from bad guys with guns,
Wish it were true
But it simply isn't.

Good guys with guns
Just as afraid
As good people without guns.

Don't have much to say
As children die in their seats,
Those of color die in the streets.

But I surmise
What we are seeing.
Is the end of the proverbial slippery slope?

No age rules,
No training requirement,
No background checks,
No red flags.
Lead us down
The wrong path
Down a slippery slope.

Don't have much to say
As children die in their seats,
Those of color die in the streets.
Time to ski in another direction.

SANDY HOOK, NOW UVALDE

I have a lot on my mind.
My brain swells.
Don't make me think anymore.
I can't comprehend.
I can't conceive.
I see their faces -
So tiny, so sweet
So innocent and bright.

TRAITOR

Orange-headed
Shit-eating grinner
Lard-ass loser.

Bankrupt 6 times.
Married 3 times.
Impeached 2 times.
Attempted coup 1 time.

Bloated belly
Foreign to telling truth
Weak-minded strongman
Selling secrets to who knows where.

Bankrupt 6 times.
Married 3 times.
Impeached 2 times.
Attempted coup 1 time.

A losing fool
Who thinks he's still in control.
A wannabee dictator
Followed by minions of deplorables.

Orange-headed
Shit-eating grinner
Lard-ass loser.

You know who it is
I reference
Because . . .

Only one orange-headed
Shit-eating grinner
Lard-ass loser.

I SEE BLACK

I see black.
I see brown.
I see all shades in between.
I'm not color blind.
I'm not ashamed to see color.
My strength is my vision.

I see black.
I see brown.
I see all shades in between.
I see therefore I learn.
I see therefore I feel.
I see therefore I include.
I see therefore I respect.

I see black.
I see brown.
I see all shades in between.
I cannot deny my eyes.
They see the pain.
They see the suffering.
They see the failure of our shared history.

I see black.
I see brown.
I see all shades in between.
I see the struggle that continues.
Repeated on a time continuum.
Not left behind.
Renewed with a different name.

AUTOBIOGRAPHY

Massachusetts on my mind.
In waves, my thoughts go to Water Street.
The constant push and pull
Where do I need to go?
Where do I want to be?

Massachusetts on my mind.
Like an odyssey on Homer Street.
The end of a beginning
Wondering how to move on.
Wondering who to turn to.

Massachusetts on my mind.
A throw from Stoneham Road.
Much of my childhood
Spent on the white cliffs.
Spent sheltered in beaver dam.

Massachusetts on my mind.
A thread through Wormtown.
From Blithewood to Rice Square
To East Middle to Forest Grove
To the Highlanders to the Lancers.

Massachusetts on my mind.
Stoic New Englander
With a heart of mush
Q'd to 'AAF
Sending a story through the Telegram.

Massachusetts on my mind.
Rekindled by the next generation.
Passing on the nostalgia
Hoping for the best as he navigates.
Hoping for the best as he investigates.

LET FREEDOM WRING

One always hears
In the music we tune to
That the male and female alike
Aren't happy without each other.
But why do they complain?
If they didn't want to live apart,
Then why did they break it off?
This is too much of a resounding sound.
Before hooking up, one always praises.
When together, each other curses.
Why not let it rest?
Start from scratch.
Purge the past from the present.
Sit back and relax!
And let the freedom wring!

'20

'20 reminiscent of '18
People dying
By the hundreds of thousands.

Taken ill by '20
Much like in '18
No lessons learned.

History of '18
Repeated during '20
No mandates, no vaccines
How many could have been saved?

APOLOGIES

We didn't save the world.
Our apologies.
We made it worse.
Our apologies.
Wasn't what we planned.
Our apologies.
We didn't do what we said we would.
Our apologies.
We handed off a bigger mess.
Our apologies.

SAME COIN

Rock
Anchor
Brick

They offer support.
And they can drag you down.

Rock
Anchor
Brick

They offer stability.
And they can destabilize.

Rock
Anchor
Brick

They provide strength.
And they can weigh you down.

Rock
Anchor
Brick

Two sides
Of the same coin.

SON OF MINE

Think before you do
Was the mantra.
Different from do as I say,
Not as I do.

I don't want you
To make the same mistakes
I made.
You have your own to make.
Make the most of them.

THREE DADS

One went in spring.
One went in winter.
One went in fall.

Real Dad
Far from easy
But better than many.
Dad died when I was twelve
A flag furled on my lap.

He tried the best he could
Like many he had limits.
Could only go so far.
Always in for a good time.

Sudden scarcity.
Quickly and far too soon.
Left the hard work for others.
But still the first Dad.

Uncle Richie
Took over for a time.
Played the father figure
Sometimes better than the first.
No complaints, just thoughtful praise.

Suffered in the end
A different man he became.
Loss of dignity, maybe.
The respect remains.

Support during the angst
Sometimes more than his own.
Drifting away was my sin.
But still the second Dad.

Dave
A man of wisdom
A man of many accomplishments
A man adored by many
A man of all people.

Reflection on my soul
Grateful for his being
Teaching grace
While leaving space.
No doubt where he was headed
Once he succumbed.
Off to a better place.
But still the third Dad.

Three Dads
Each had their influence.
Each left their mark.
Each lives within me.
Throughout the many seasons.

NO REGRETS

No regrets,
No belief.

No mistakes,
Nothing to take back,
Nothing to say sorry for.

No truths,
No lies,
No holding back,
Until the right time.

No bad decisions,
No wrong answers,
No selling one short,
No raising someone up.

No letting go,
No compromising,
No setting the record straight,
When it needed it to be.

No praying to God,
No wishing for a blessing,
No seeking someone else's help,
When that's all you needed.

No possibility of redemption,
No signs of salvation,
No chance of peace
No disruption in life.

No regrets,
No way,
No how,
Too easy to whitewash.

RIGHT AND WRONG SPEECH

Fiercely independent.
Don't want to be told
What to do
Until it's time to tell someone else
What to do.

Rugged individualism
When it comes to you.

Love thy neighbor.
Love thy friend.

Hear the evangelical Christians.
I don't listen.
Not much for religion.
Not much for control.
Not much for what they are selling.

Tell people who they can't love.
Tell people what they can't teach.
Tell people how they can't parent.
Tell people what they can't read.
Tell people they can't make healthy decisions.

Playing God
When they know so little about Jesus
Preach, preach, preach.

Meanwhile they lie.
Meanwhile they kill.
Meanwhile they steal.
Meanwhile they commit adultery.
Meanwhile they cheat.
Meanwhile they molest.
Meanwhile they bear false witness.
Meanwhile they say His name in vain.

Project onto others
As you'd do unto others
The Golden Rule
Tarnished by Almighty avarice.

Playing God
When they know so little of Jesus
Preach, preach, preach.

Fiercely independent.
Don't want to be told
What to do
Until it's time to tell someone else
What to do.

HINDSIGHT

It's easy
And not so much
To look back with 20/20
Knowing everything is 50/50.

WHAT A BALL

Rolling down a hill
I keep accumulating
Things I don't need.
Things people left behind.
Trash and debris
That fill my mind.
The faster it moves,
The faster it grows,
Gravitational acceleration
No force too strong
To stop it
Until it hits a plateau.

ANOTHER HO HUM DAY

In a hum drum life.
Wouldn't want it
Any other way.

An uneventful day.
No drama to be had.
Wouldn't want it
Any other way.

Boring as it seems
The stillness brings respite.
Wouldn't want it
Any other way.

LOST BOYS

Too many slaps on the wrist.
Too many betrayed plot twists.
Nobody can describe
How it feels
When two boys, twelve and eleven
Are allowed to make adult decisions
In a circuit of lies and deceit.

BEST LOVE SONG

I saw her walking
In those black boots
Not quite go-gos
But they made me go-go.

I wasn't in the best of places
But in a leading way we met.
We traveled roads
Across scenic Carolina
Initially not into each other's arms.

Then you came to my aide
When I was looking the other way.
Pigs weren't flying
But running at the fair.

Kyrie brought us together
In the cathedral of your dreams.
You soon became
The champion of my heart.

I've had my share of loves
None so everlasting
None so unconditional
Maybe because
You are my best love song.

WHORE-IFYING

Sell out
For fame.
Sell out
For pay.
Sell out
For power.

Show a little leg
For a lot of money.

Flash a little skin
For a lot of notoriety.

Say something incendiary
To ignite a fire.

Put everything together
To create a personal industry.

Good for one
Not good for many.

Whore-ifying positions,
But not to worry.
I got mine.
Do you want yours?

THE MOMENT

Sit.
Think.
Take it all in.

Breathe.
Behold.
Take it all in.

Touch.
Feel.
Take it all in.

Taste.
Savor.
Take it all in.

Enjoy the moment.
For it too shall pass.
Take it all in.

BRIDGES AND ARCS

We are still working
On building the bridge
Between our lives.
Sometimes I feel
Like waving from the side
As a passerby.

Two sides of an arc
Meeting in the middle
Buttressing each other.
The apex of the circle
Separated by a thin line.

RESIDUALS

The house was quiet
As you were cruising on the high seas.
Where were the kids?
All just a blur.
Something unexpected
Came in the mail that day.
A notice it was over.
You had shipped out.

I tried calling shore to ship.
Tried to get answers
From dead salt air.

The truck pulled up
Not long thereafter.
She pulled up stakes
Right through my heart.

The washer almost went
As she cleansed herself
From my life.
Where were the kids?
They knew before me
How clouded I must have been.

CROSSFIRE

I'm sorry
For what we did to you.
Putting you in the middle
Did we do it out of love?
We told ourselves that,
But love was the last thing
We had for one another.
It showed
And you saw it.
How could you not?
We tugged you like a rope
Back and forth.
While you hung over the pit
Like a flag
Dangling in the wind.

MURAL

No mural to this story.
Larger than life images
Suspended between two states.
On the sides of buildings
On both sides of the street.

Protests.
Tributes.
Art.
Profound words.

Depictions of suffering.
Portraits of pain.
Celebrations of hope.
Symbols of conscience.

Signs of the times
Ways of life
A stitch in time
In a thoughtful design.

No mural to this story.
Larger than life images
Suspended between two states.
On the sides of buildings
On both sides of the street.

CLUB

I still see the image.
A little man
In a little graduation gown.
On a small stage
With robe of green and tassle.

What do you want to be when you grow up?
A Power Ranger!

Who do you see in the crowd?
That's my dad!

Welling with tears
In full pride
Refreshed at life's milestones.
And grows over time.

I still see the images.
From club to college and forward.
Oh, how you've grown!

PERCENT OF FOREVER

Percent of forever
Is all I need.
Not one hundred percent
Just a taste.
A nip of intoxication.
A buzz of your being.
Not asking for more
Don't want to overdo it.
No need to get greedy.
Give me your happiness.
Give me a percent of your forever.

EXPIRATION DATE

Expiration date is coming.
Could be today.
Could be tomorrow.
Could be five minutes away.
Could be five years from now.

Expiration date is coming.
No last sell-by date.
No spoilage.
No rancid meat.

Expiration date is coming.
Not overstaying my welcome.
Put me to bed quietly
For the long sleep.

Printed in the USA
CPSIA information can be obtained
at www.ICGtesting.com
JSHW020455120524
62884JS00005B/155